D1605342

SYMBOLS of AMERICA

The Declaration of Independence

UPPER SADDLE RIVER LIBRARY
245 LAKE ST.
UPPER SADDLE RIVER, NJ 07458

Terry Allan Hicks

mc **Marshall Cavendish**
Benchmark

Marshall Cavendish Benchmark
99 White Plains Road
Tarrytown, New York 10591-9001
www.marshallcavendish.us

© 2007 by Marshall Cavendish Corporation

All rights reserved. No part of this book may be reproduced or utilized in any form or by any
means electronic or mechanical, including photocopying, recording, or by any information
storage and retrieval system, without permission from the copyright holders.

All Web sites were available and accurate when this book was sent to press.

Library of Congress Cataloging-in-Publication Data
Hicks, Terry Allan.
The Declaration of Independence / by Terry Allan Hicks.
p. cm. — (Symbols of America)
Summary: "An exploration of the origins, history, and content of this historical document
that has become an important American symbol" —Provided by publisher.
Includes bibliographical references (p. 38) and index.
ISBN-13: 978-0-7614-2135-1
ISBN-10: 0-7614-2135-1
1. United States. Declaration of Independence—Juvenile literature. 2. United States—Politics and
government—1775-1783—Juvenile literature. I. Title. II. Series: Hicks, Terry Allan. Symbols of America.

E221.H55 2006
973.3'13—dc22
2005020611 @LS:

Photo research by Anne Burns Images

Front cover photo: Corbis/Ted Spiegel
Back cover photo: U. S. Postal Service

The photographs in this book are used by permission and through the courtesy of: *Corbis:* Jose Luis Pelaez, Inc., 1; Joseph
Sohm, 4; Richard T. Nowitz, 7, 32; Royalty Free, 8; Poodles Rock, 19; John Henley, 25; Bettman, 27. *North Wind Picture
Archives:* 11, 12, 15, 20, 24, 31. *The Granger Collection:* 16, 23, 28.

Series design by Adam Mietlowski

Printed in Malaysia

1 3 5 6 4 2

Contents

CHAPTER ONE

America's Birth Certificate

Every year, on July 4, people across the United States celebrate *Independence* Day. With parades and speeches, picnics and fireworks, Americans show the pride they have in their nation. These celebrations mark the day, more than 225 years ago, when a very important *document* was signed.

It is the Declaration of Independence, sometimes called "America's birth certificate."

Marchers in Revolutionary War costumes mark a special day in American history at a Fourth of July parade.

On July 4, 1776, the delegates to the Second Continental Congress voted to approve the Declaration of Independence. They had come together *representing* the people of the thirteen colonies. The declaration stated, in simple yet powerful language, that the American people had the right to choose their own government. It is this freedom to choose that Americans honor on the Fourth of July.

Many of the people of the colonies were angry with their British rulers. They were unhappy with what they saw as harsh laws and unfair taxes. They had waited for many years for the British king, George III, to listen to their complaints. By the time the Second Continental Congress met, they were no longer willing to wait.

The Declaration of Independence. This important document stated America's claims to freedom and the right to rule itself. ▶

IN CONGRESS. July 4, 1776.

The unanimous Declaration of the thirteen united States of America.

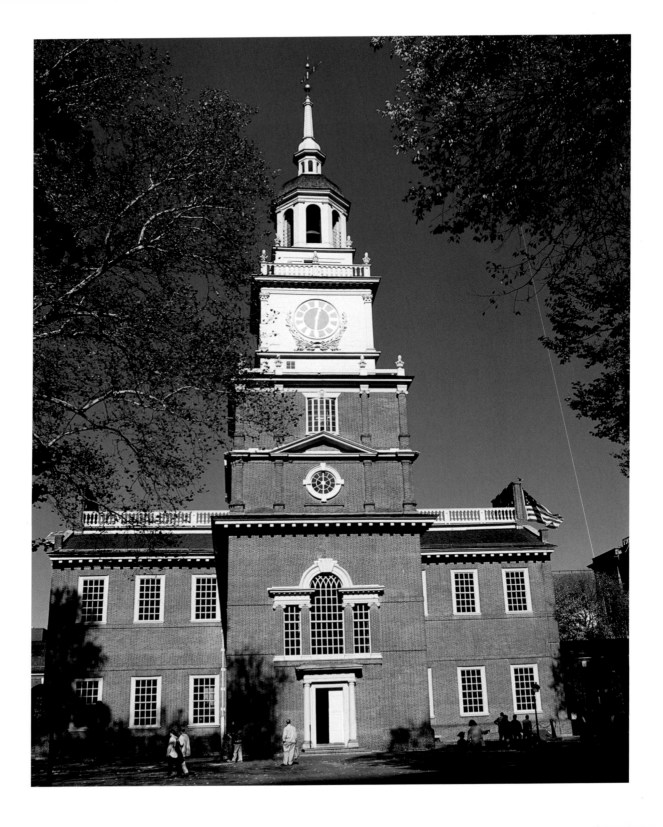

The Second Continental Congress first met on May 10, 1775. The delegates gathered in the Pennsylvania State House in Philadelphia, which is now known as Independence Hall. They had come together to present their complaints to the king. It was not the first time. The Stamp Act Congress had taken place in 1765 to oppose a harsh series of taxes. The First Continental Congress had met in 1774. But the British had ignored the colonists' demand for change. So the colonists were getting ready for war.

◀ *The delegates gathered for their important meetings at what is today called Independence Hall, in Philadelphia.*

In fact, the war had already begun. Less than a month earlier, on April 19, *minutemen* had fought with British soldiers in the Massachusetts towns of Lexington and Concord. In the following months, battles took place at Bunker Hill and Fort Ticonderoga. Even as the delegates discussed the Declaration of Independence, a British army was closing in on the city of Boston.

The Americans lost the battle of Bunker Hill, but they proved they could stand up ▶
to the powerful British forces, known for their red uniforms.

On June 7, 1776, as the fighting continued, Richard Henry Lee of Virginia rose in the State House and presented a *resolution*. It began:

Resolved: That these United Colonies are, and of right ought to be, free and independent States . . .

On June 11, the Congress, expecting the Lee Resolution to be approved, created the Committee of Five. This was a group of delegates chosen to prepare a *draft* of the Declaration of Independence. The committee included John Adams of Massachusetts, Benjamin Franklin of Pennsylvania, Robert Livingston of New York, and Roger Sherman of Connecticut. The fifth member was the one who would actually write the Declaration of Independence—a brilliant young man from Virginia named Thomas Jefferson.

◀ *The Committee of Five meets to discuss the proper wording of the Declaration of Independence.*

CHAPTER TWO

A Place of Honor

It was not surprising that the Committee of Five chose Thomas Jefferson to write the Declaration of Independence. The young Virginian—then just thirty-three years old—was well-known for his many talents, including his skill as a writer.

Jefferson returned to his rented rooms, in a house owned by a bricklayer named Jacob Graff. There, complaining of the summer heat and the horseflies drawn to a nearby stable, he began writing his draft of the Declaration of Independence.

Many people believe Thomas Jefferson was one of the most gifted presidents to be elected to that office. ▶

Thomas Jefferson's greatest *inspiration* was probably the work of George Mason, who had written a "declaration of *rights*" for the Virginia *legislature*. Many of Mason's ideas were later used in the first ten amendments to the United States Constitution, which we know as the Bill of Rights.

Did You Know?

Thomas Jefferson was a writer, a lawyer, a scholar, a farmer, and a self-taught architect, inventor, and scientist. During his long career, he served as governor of Virginia, *ambassador* to France, secretary of state, and later as vice president. Then, in 1801, he became the nation's third president.

◄ *George Mason of Virginia is sometimes called the Father of the Bill of Rights.*

On June 21, Jefferson showed his draft to the other members of the Committee of Five. They made a few changes and then, on June 28, presented it to the congress. The draft contained a long list of complaints against King George III. It also boldly stated that Americans had the right to govern themselves. This idea was expressed in the declaration's most famous passage:

We hold these truths to be *self-evident*, that all men are created equal, that they are *endowed* by their Creator with certain *unalienable* Rights, that among these are Life, *Liberty* and the pursuit of Happiness.

Thomas Jefferson (right) shows Benjamin Franklin (left) and John Adams a draft of the Declaration of Independence.   ▶

THE COMMITTEE

On July 2, the delegates to the congress approved the Lee Resolution. They then began to debate the Declaration of Independence. They, too, made some changes. The most important was the removal of a statement holding George III responsible for the slave trade. Many of the delegates, including Thomas Jefferson, owned slaves. Some of them refused to sign the document if it included any criticism of slavery.

Late in the afternoon of July 4, the delegates voted on Thomas Jefferson's draft. Only the New York delegation did not vote, because its members were waiting for instructions from their state legislature. (They finally added their votes in favor of the declaration on July 9.)

This illustration shows most of the delegates who attended the Second Continental Congress.

Did You Know?

In 1776 one in every five people in the thirteen colonies was of African ancestry. Almost all of them were slaves. Slavery continued to exist in the United States long after the Declaration of Independence was signed. Slavery was not officially *outlawed* until 1865, when the states approved the Thirteenth Amendment to the Constitution.

When the declaration had been approved, it was printed on *parchment* for the delegates to sign. John Hancock of Massachusetts, the president of the congress, was the first to sign the declaration. Only Hancock and the secretary of the congress, Charles Thomson, actually signed the declaration on July 4. The other fifty-four signatures were all added later.

Did You Know?

• The first signer of the declaration became so famous that, even today, a signature is often called a "John Hancock."

• The British viewed the fifty-six signers of the Declaration of Independence as traitors. At least twelve of the signers had their homes burned during the Revolutionary War.

John Hancock boldly signed the declaration, even though the British had placed a price on his head.

And for the support
of this declaration we
mutually pledge to
each other our lives
our fortunes & our
sacred honour.

John Hancock

The declaration was then sent to a printer, who made copies to be sent to all the colonies. On the morning of July 8, 1776, John Nixon, an officer in the Continental Army, read the declaration in public for the first time. When he finished, the crowd cheered and the bells of the town began ringing loudly.

The Declaration of Independence had begun to take its place of honor in the hearts of Americans.

◀ *The first public reading of the newly printed Declaration of Independence. It was met with cheering and the ringing of bells across the city of Philadelphia.*

CHAPTER THREE

The Pursuit of Happiness

The Declaration of Independence has been an inspiration to Americans for more than two hundred years. On November 19, 1863, President Abraham Lincoln referred to the Declaration of Independence in the Gettysburg Address. In this famous speech, made at the height of the Civil War, he said:

> Four score and seven [eighty-seven] years ago, our fathers brought forth upon this continent a new nation: conceived in liberty, and dedicated to the proposition [idea] that all men are created equal.

Abraham Lincoln delivers his important speech, the Gettysburg Address. ▶

Lincoln was answering the question that had troubled Thomas Jefferson and many of the other signers of the Declaration of Independence: Were all Americans—including those of African descent—truly equal? In this speech, just months after he signed the *Emancipation Proclamation*, Lincoln said, very clearly, that they were. No Americans, whatever their racial background, would ever be enslaved again.

The 1862 Emancipation Proclamation freed all the slaves living in the Southern states.

Did You Know?

Americans are not the only people who have been moved by the Declaration of Independence. In 1789, the French, rebelling against their king, issued a statement that echoed Thomas Jefferson's words: "Men are born free and equal in rights . . ." Almost two hundred years later, the Japanese, after their defeat in World War Two, *adopted* a new constitution. It referred to the rights of "life, liberty, and the pursuit of happiness."

The Declaration of Independence is one of America's most precious historical documents. But it has not always been treated with the respect it deserves. The original declaration was nearly destroyed during the War of 1812, when British soldiers burned much of Washington, D.C. A clerk at the Department of State, Stephen Pleasanton, rescued the parchment and many other valuable documents, hiding them until the war was over.

During the War of 1812, British soldiers burned many of Washington, D.C.'s, most important buildings. ▶

IN CONGRESS. JULY 4, 1776.

The unanimous Declaration of the thirteen united States of America.

When in the Course of human events, it becomes necessary for one people to dissolve the political bands which have connected them with another, and to assume among the powers of the earth, the separate and equal station to which the Laws of Nature and of Nature's God entitle them, a decent respect to the opinions of mankind requires that they should declare the causes which impel them to the separation.

We hold these truths to be self-evident, that all men are created equal, that they are endowed by their Creator with certain unalienable Rights, that among these are Life, Liberty and the pursuit of Happiness. — That to secure these rights, Governments are instituted among Men, deriving their just powers from the consent of the governed, — That whenever any Form of Government becomes destructive of these ends, it is the Right of the People to alter or to abolish it, and to institute new Government, laying its foundation on such principles and organizing its powers in such form, as to them shall seem most likely to effect their Safety and Happiness. Prudence, indeed, will dictate that Governments long established should not be changed for light and transient causes; and accordingly all experience hath shewn, that mankind are more disposed to suffer, while evils are sufferable, than to right themselves by abolishing the forms to which they are accustomed. But when a long train of abuses and usurpations, pursuing invariably the same Object evinces a design to reduce them under absolute Despotism, it is their right, it is their duty, to throw off such Government, and to provide new Guards for their future security. — Such has been the patient sufferance of these Colonies; and such is now the necessity which constrains them to alter their former Systems of Government. The history of the present King of Great Britain is a history of repeated injuries and usurpations, all having in direct object the establishment of an absolute Tyranny over these States. To prove this, let Facts be submitted to a candid world.

He has refused his Assent to Laws, the most wholesome and necessary for the public good.

He has forbidden his Governors to pass Laws of immediate and pressing importance, unless suspended in their operation till his Assent should be obtained; and when so suspended, he has utterly neglected to attend to them.

He has refused to pass other Laws for the accommodation of large districts of people, unless those people would relinquish the right of Representation in the Legislature, a right inestimable to them and formidable to tyrants only.

He has called together legislative bodies at places unusual, uncomfortable, and distant from the depository of their public Records, for the sole purpose of fatiguing them into compliance with his measures.

He has dissolved Representative Houses repeatedly, for opposing with manly firmness his invasions on the rights of the people.

He has refused for a long time, after such dissolutions, to cause others to be elected; whereby the Legislative powers, incapable of Annihilation, have returned to the People at large for their exercise; the State remaining in the mean time exposed to all the dangers of invasion from without, and convulsions within.

He has endeavoured to prevent the population of these States; for that purpose obstructing the Laws for Naturalization of Foreigners; refusing to pass others to encourage their migrations hither, and raising the conditions of new Appropriations of Lands.

He has obstructed the Administration of Justice, by refusing his Assent to Laws for establishing Judiciary powers.

He has made Judges dependent on his Will alone, for the tenure of their offices, and the amount and payment of their salaries.

He has erected a multitude of New Offices, and sent hither swarms of Officers to harrass our people, and eat out their substance.

He has kept among us, in times of peace, Standing Armies without the Consent of our legislatures.

He has affected to render the Military independent of and superior to the Civil power.

He has combined with others to subject us to a jurisdiction foreign to our constitution, and unacknowledged by our laws; giving his Assent to their Acts of pretended Legislation:

For Quartering large bodies of armed troops among us:

For protecting them, by a mock Trial, from punishment for any Murders which they should commit on the Inhabitants of these States:

For cutting off our Trade with all parts of the world:

For imposing Taxes on us without our Consent:

For depriving us in many cases, of the benefits of Trial by Jury:

For transporting us beyond Seas to be tried for pretended offences:

For abolishing the free System of English Laws in a neighbouring Province, establishing therein an Arbitrary government, and enlarging its Boundaries so as to render it at once an example and fit instrument for introducing the same absolute rule into these Colonies:

For taking away our Charters, abolishing our most valuable Laws, and altering fundamentally the Forms of our Governments:

For suspending our own Legislatures, and declaring themselves invested with power to legislate for us in all cases whatsoever.

He has abdicated Government here, by declaring us out of his Protection and waging War against us.

He has plundered our seas, ravaged our Coasts, burnt our towns, and destroyed the lives of our people.

He is at this time transporting large Armies of foreign Mercenaries to compleat the works of death, desolation and tyranny, already begun with circumstances of Cruelty & perfidy scarcely paralleled in the most barbarous ages, and totally unworthy the Head of a civilized nation.

He has constrained our fellow Citizens taken Captive on the high Seas to bear Arms against their Country, to become the executioners of their friends and Brethren, or to fall themselves by their Hands.

He has excited domestic insurrections amongst us, and has endeavoured to bring on the inhabitants of our frontiers, the merciless Indian Savages, whose known rule of warfare, is an undistinguished destruction of all ages, sexes and conditions.

In every stage of these Oppressions We have Petitioned for Redress in the most humble terms: Our repeated Petitions have been answered only by repeated injury. A Prince, whose character is thus marked by every act which may define a Tyrant, is unfit to be the ruler of a free people.

Nor have We been wanting in attentions to our British brethren. We have warned them from time to time of attempts by their legislature to extend an unwarrantable jurisdiction over us. We have reminded them of the circumstances of our emigration and settlement here. We have appealed to their native justice and magnanimity, and we have conjured them by the ties of our common kindred to disavow these usurpations, which, would inevitably interrupt our connections and correspondence. They too have been deaf to the voice of justice and of consanguinity. We must, therefore, acquiesce in the necessity, which denounces our Separation, and hold them, as we hold the rest of mankind, Enemies in War, in Peace Friends.

We, therefore, the Representatives of the united States of America, in General Congress, Assembled, appealing to the Supreme Judge of the world for the rectitude of our intentions, do, in the Name, and by Authority of the good People of these Colonies, solemnly publish and declare, That these United Colonies are, and of Right ought to be Free and Independent States; that they are Absolved from all Allegiance to the British Crown, and that all political connection between them and the State of Great Britain, is and ought to be totally dissolved; and that as Free and Independent States, they have full Power to levy War, conclude Peace, contract Alliances, establish Commerce, and to do all other Acts and Things which Independent States may of right do. — And for the support of this Declaration, with a firm reliance on the protection of Divine Providence, we mutually pledge to each other our Lives, our Fortunes and our sacred Honor.

John Hancock

Button Gwinnett
Lyman Hall
Geo Walton.

Wm Hooper
Joseph Hewes
John Penn

Edward Rutledge.

Thos Heyward Junr.
Thomas Lynch Junr.
Arthur Middleton

Samuel Chase
Wm Paca
Thos Stone
Charles Carroll of Carrollton

George Wythe
Richard Henry Lee
Th Jefferson
Benja Harrison
Thos Nelson jr.
Francis Lightfoot Lee
Carter Braxton

Robt Morris
Benjamin Rush
Benja Franklin
John Morton
Geo Clymer
Jas Smith
Geo Taylor
James Wilson
Geo. Ross
Caesar Rodney
Geo Read
Tho M:Kean

Wm Floyd
Phil. Livingston
Frans Lewis
Lewis Morris

Richd Stockton
Jno Witherspoon
Fras Hopkinson
John Hart
Abra Clark

Josiah Bartlett
Wm Whipple
Saml Adams
John Adams
Robt Treat Paine
Elbridge Gerry
Step Hopkins
William Ellery
Roger Sherman
Sam: Huntington
Wm Williams
Oliver Wolcott
Matthew Thornton

By 1823 the ink was already fading on the document, so a *facsimile* was printed. This is the version of the declaration that most people know today. From 1841 to 1876, the parchment hung on a wall at the United States Patent Office, where sunlight caused it to fade even more. In 1876, the declaration was taken to Philadelphia. It was shown to the crowds at the Centennial National Exposition, an event honoring America's one hundredth birthday.

Today, the document is cracked and faded, but still readable. It is *preserved,* with the greatest possible care, in the National Archives building in Washington, D.C.

◀ *The 1823 facsimile or copy of the Declaration of Independence.*

The simple yet powerful ideas contained in the Declaration of Independence have guided the United States for more than two hundred years. The words Thomas Jefferson wrote in his rented rooms in Philadelphia so many years ago still echo around the world. They will continue to do so as long as people prize the right to life, liberty, and the pursuit of happiness.

A day for fun, people all over the country celebrate "America's birthday," the ▶
Fourth of July, in their own special ways.

Glossary

adopt—To accept a decision or a course of action.

ambassador—A person who represents his or her country.

document—A written or printed statement.

draft—A version of a document that may be changed later.

Emancipation Proclamation—An order by President Abraham Lincoln freeing all slaves held in the Southern states.

endow—To give, grant, or provide with.

facsimile—An exact copy.

independence—Freedom.

inspiration—Something that moves or excites people.

legislature—The part of a government that creates laws.

liberty—Freedom.

minutemen—American patriots sworn to fight the British "at a minute's notice."

outlaw—To make something illegal.

parchment—An animal skin (or sometimes a paper) that can be written on.

preserve—To keep something safe from harm.

represent—To act in place of someone else.

resolution—A course of action that people have decided to follow.

right—A freedom or ability that people are granted or entitled to.

self-evident—True, that which does not need to be proved.

unalienable—That which cannot be taken away; more commonly used today in the form *inalienable*.

Find Out More

Books

Fink, Sam. *The Declaration of Independence.* New York: Scholastic, 2002.

Fradin, Dennis Brindell. *The Signers: The 56 Stories behind the Declaration of Independence.* New York: Walker, 2003.

Freedman, Russell. *Give Me Liberty: The Story of the Declaration of Independence.* New York: Holiday House, 2002.

Oberle, Lora Polack. *The Declaration of Independence.* Mankato, MN: Bridgestone, 2002.

Pierce, Alan. *The Declaration of Independence.* Edina, MN: Abdo, 2004.

Quiri, Patricia Ryon. *The Declaration of Independence.* Danbury, CT: Children's Press, 1999.

Web Sites

America's Freedom Documents
http://earlyamerica.com/earlyamerica/freedom/

Declaration of Independence Quiz
http://www.whitehouse.gov/kids/dec_indep/quiz/

Declaring Independence: Drafting the Documents
http://www.loc.gov/exhibits/declara/declara1.html

In Congress, July 4, 1776
http://www.kidsdomain.com/holiday/july4/decl.html

Thomas Jefferson—Declaration of Independence
http://www.loc.gov/exhibits/jefferson/jeffdec.html

Index

DATE DUE

9/66